A GUIDE TO NURTURING MENTAL HEALTH

Embracing the journey

OKAFOR EMMANUEL ONYEDIKA

DEDICATION

This book is dedicated to my family and everyone out there looking for ways to improve their mental health and well-being.

CONTENTS

INTRODUCTION

Welcome to "Embracing the Journey: A Guide to Nurturing Mental Health and Well-Being." In this book, we embark on an insightful exploration of mental health and well-being, aiming to empower readers with the knowledge and tools to foster a healthier and happier life. We understand that mental health is a crucial aspect of overall well-being, and by addressing it with compassion and understanding, we can lead more fulfilling lives and build a more empathetic society. Whether you are seeking ways to enhance your own mental well-being or looking to support a loved one, this comprehensive guide will provide valuable insights and practical strategies to navigate the journey toward mental wellness.

UNDERSTANDING MENTAL HEALTH

Mental health can be defined as a state of well-being in which an individual realizes their own potential, can cope with the normal stresses of life, work productively, and make meaningful contributions to their community. It encompasses emotional, psychological, and social aspects of a person's life and is an essential component of overall health and well-being.

Importance of Mental Health in Everyday Life

Emotional Well-Being: Mental health influences how we experience and manage our emotions. Being mentally healthy allows us to understand and express our feelings in a constructive manner, leading to better emotional regulation and resilience in the face of challenges.

Cognitive Functioning: A sound mental state is vital for cognitive processes such as learning, memory, problem-solving, and decision-making. When mentally healthy, our cognitive abilities are optimized, enabling us to process information effectively and make informed choices.

Physical Health: Mental health and physical health are interconnected. Mental health issues can contribute to physical health problems, such as weakened immune function, increased risk of chronic diseases, and slower recovery from illnesses.

Relationships: Strong mental health positively impacts our ability to form and maintain healthy relationships with others. It allows us to communicate effectively, empathize, and establish meaningful connections, contributing to a supportive and fulfilling social life.

Coping with Stress: Life is full of stressors, both big and small. Good mental health equips us with coping mechanisms to manage stress effectively, reducing its negative impact on our physical and emotional well-being. Productivity and Performance: Mental health influences our capacity to focus, concentrate, and be productive in various aspects of life, including work, education, and hobbies.

Self-Esteem and Self-Confidence: Positive mental health fosters a healthy self-esteem and self-confidence, enabling us to recognize our worth and believe in our abilities.

Adaptability and Resilience: Mental health enables us to adapt to changes and bounce back from setbacks, demonstrating resilience in the face of adversity.

Overall Quality of Life: When our mental health is well-cared for, we are more likely to experience an improved overall quality of life, with greater life satisfaction and happiness.

Reducing Stigma: Prioritizing mental health in everyday life helps break the stigma surrounding mental health challenges. Openly discussing mental health normalizes seeking help and support when needed.

Promoting Mental Health in Everyday Life

Self-Care: Engage in activities that promote relaxation, joy, and emotional well-being, such as exercise, hobbies, spending time in nature, or practicing mindfulness.

Healthy Relationships: Nourish positive relationships with family, friends, and colleagues by maintaining open communication, empathy, and understanding.

Seeking Support: If facing challenges, don't hesitate to seek support from mental health professionals or support groups. Seeking help is a sign of strength and self-awareness.

Balancing Work and Life: Strive for a healthy work-life balance, allowing time for leisure, rest, and self-reflection.

Practicing Mindfulness: Incorporate mindfulness practices into daily life to increase awareness of thoughts and emotions, and reduce stress.

Avoiding Substance Abuse: Refrain from using drugs or alcohol as coping mechanisms, as they can exacerbate mental health issues.

Educating Yourself and Others: Stay informed about mental health and share knowledge with others to help reduce stigma and increase understanding.

Debunking common myths and misconceptions surrounding mental health

Debunking common myths and misconceptions surrounding mental health is crucial for promoting understanding, empathy, and support for individuals facing mental health challenges. Let's address some of these myths and clarify the facts:

Myth 1: Mental health issues are rare and uncommon.
Fact: Mental health issues are prevalent worldwide. According to the World Health Organization (WHO), approximately 1 in 4 people will experience a mental health problem at some point in their lives. Mental health challenges can affect anyone regardless of age, gender, ethnicity, or socioeconomic status.

Myth 2: Mental health issues are a sign of weakness or lack of character.
Fact: Mental health challenges are not a reflection of weakness or character flaws. They are medical conditions influenced by various factors, including genetics, environment, and life experiences. Just like physical health issues, mental health conditions require understanding and support.

Myth 3: People with mental health issues are violent and dangerous.
Fact: The vast majority of individuals with mental health issues are not violent or dangerous. In reality, they are more likely to be victims of violence or self-harm. Most individuals with mental health challenges are non-violent and pose no threat to others.

Myth 4: Children do not experience mental health problems.
Fact: Children and adolescents can also experience mental health issues. Conditions like anxiety, depression, and attention deficit hyperactivity disorder (ADHD) can affect young people, and early intervention is crucial to supporting

their well-being.

Myth 5: You can simply "snap out of" a mental health condition.
Fact: Mental health conditions are not something a person can just "snap out of" or overcome with willpower alone. These conditions often require professional treatment, support, and time for recovery.

Myth 6: Seeking help for mental health issues is a sign of weakness.
Fact: Seeking help for mental health challenges is a sign of strength and self-awareness. Just like seeking medical assistance for physical ailments, reaching out for mental health support is essential for recovery and well-being.

Myth 7: Only traumatic events can trigger mental health issues.
Fact: While trauma can certainly be a trigger for some mental health conditions, there is a wide range of factors that can contribute to mental health challenges. Biological factors, genetics, family history, and life stressors can all play a role.

Myth 8: Medications are the only treatment for mental health issues.
Fact: While medications can be an essential part of treatment for some individuals, they are not the only approach. Therapy, counseling, support groups, lifestyle changes, and self-care practices are also effective in managing mental health conditions.

Myth 9: Mental health conditions are life-long and cannot improve.
Fact: With proper treatment, support, and coping strategies, many people with mental health conditions can experience significant improvement and lead fulfilling lives.

Myth 10: You can't help someone with a mental health issue unless you are a professional.
Fact: Support from friends, family, and the community is essential for individuals facing mental health challenges. Simple acts of kindness, empathy, and non-judgmental listening can make a significant difference in someone's recovery journey.

By dispelling these myths and promoting accurate information, we can create a more understanding and compassionate society that supports individuals experiencing mental health challenges. Education and open dialogue are powerful tools in reducing stigma and fostering an environment where seeking help for mental health is encouraged and normalized.

The connection between mental health and physical well-being

The connection between mental health and physical well-being is profound and bidirectional. It is often described as the mind-body connection, where the state of our mental health can significantly impact our physical health, and vice versa. Let's explore this connection in more detail:

Impact of Mental Health on Physical Health

Immune System: Chronic stress and mental health issues can weaken the immune system, making individuals more susceptible to infections and illnesses.

Cardiovascular Health: Conditions like anxiety and depression can contribute to increased heart rate, blood pressure, and inflammation, affecting cardiovascular health.

Sleep Patterns: Mental health challenges can disrupt sleep patterns, leading to insomnia or poor sleep quality, which, in turn, negatively impacts overall physical health.

Chronic Pain: Mental health issues can exacerbate chronic pain conditions, making them more challenging to manage. Digestive Health: Stress and anxiety can affect digestion, leading to gastrointestinal issues like irritable bowel syndrome (IBS).

Hormonal Imbalances: Mental health conditions can influence hormone levels, potentially affecting various bodily functions.

Impact of Physical Health on Mental Health

Pain and Discomfort: Chronic physical conditions can lead to emotional distress, anxiety, and depression due to ongoing pain and discomfort.

Limitations and Disabilities: Physical disabilities or limitations may impact a person's self-esteem and lead to mental health challenges.

Lifestyle Factors: Physical health conditions may require lifestyle adjustments, which can affect a person's mental well-being, leading to stress or frustration.

Medication Side Effects: Some medications used to treat physical health conditions can have side effects that impact mental health.

Coping Mechanisms

Physical Activity: Regular exercise is not only beneficial for physical health but also has positive effects on mental well-being, reducing stress and promoting a sense of well-being.

Relaxation Techniques: Practices like mindfulness, yoga, and meditation can alleviate mental stress and improve physical relaxation.

Social Interaction: Engaging in physical activities with others can boost social connections and enhance mental health.

Healthy Eating: A balanced diet plays a crucial role in supporting both physical and mental health.

Shared Biological Pathways

Neurotransmitters: Many neurotransmitters that regulate mood and emotions in the brain are also involved in regulating bodily functions, demonstrating the close interaction between the brain and body.

Inflammation: Chronic inflammation, which can arise from physical health conditions, has been linked to an increased risk of developing mental health disorders.

Psychological Factors

Perception of Illness: A person's mental state can influence how they perceive and cope with physical health conditions.

Coping Strategies: Mental health influences a person's ability to cope with physical health challenges and adhere to treatment plans.

Recognizing the interplay between mental health and physical well-being underscores the importance of a holistic approach to health care. Treating mental health and physical health as interconnected aspects of overall well-being can lead to better outcomes for individuals facing various health challenges. Integrating mental health support into physical health care and vice versa can improve patient well-being and enhance the overall quality of life. Moreover, adopting healthy lifestyle practices that promote both mental and physical health contributes to a more balanced and fulfilling life.

THE SPECTRUM OF MENTAL HEALTH

Exploring the continuum of mental health, from flourishing to struggling

The continuum of mental health represents a spectrum that ranges from flourishing to struggling. It reflects the varying degrees of mental well-being and encompasses different states that individuals may experience throughout their lives. Let's explore the different points on this continuum:

Flourishing: At the flourishing end of the continuum, individuals experience optimal mental health and well-being. They demonstrate resilience, positive emotions, and a sense of purpose in life. Flourishing individuals tend to have a strong support system, good self-esteem, and the ability to cope effectively with life's challenges. They have a positive outlook on life, maintain healthy relationships, and feel a sense of fulfillment and satisfaction in their daily activities.

Thriving: Thriving individuals fall within the higher end of the continuum and exhibit positive mental health, but they may occasionally face minor challenges. They experience a generally positive mood and can effectively manage stressors and setbacks. Thriving individuals may have a few areas of concern but overall maintain a high level of well-being.

Coping: Individuals in the coping stage experience some challenges and stressors that may affect their mental health but are still able to manage these difficulties. They may seek support from friends, family, or professionals to help them navigate through tough times. Coping individuals may have moments of emotional distress but are generally resilient in handling life's ups and downs.

 Struggling: The struggling phase includes individuals facing more significant mental health challenges. They might experience symptoms of anxiety, depression, or other mental health conditions that impact their daily functioning. At this stage, seeking professional support and intervention is essential to manage and improve mental well-being.

Crisis: The crisis stage represents a severe decline in mental health, where individuals may experience intense emotional turmoil and struggle to cope with their emotions and circumstances. Crisis situations often require immediate intervention, such as hospitalization or crisis hotlines, to ensure the person's safety and well-being.

Severe Mental Illness: At the extreme end of the continuum, individuals may suffer from severe and persistent mental health conditions such as schizophrenia or bipolar disorder. These conditions can significantly impair functioning and require ongoing treatment, support, and management.

It's important to recognize that individuals may move back and forth along this continuum throughout their lives. Factors such as life events, stressors, support systems, and self-care practices can influence a person's position on the mental health continuum.

Promoting Mental Health and Well-Being

i. Raise awareness and reduce stigma surrounding mental health challenges.
ii. Encourage open conversations about mental health to support those struggling.
iii. Promote self-care practices, mindfulness, and stress reduction techniques for better mental well-being.
iv. Advocate for accessible and affordable mental health services to provide timely support and intervention.

v.   Foster a supportive and empathetic environment that encourages seeking help without judgment.

vi.   Educate individuals on recognizing the signs of mental health challenges in themselves and others.

By understanding the continuum of mental health and providing appropriate support at each stage, we can create a more compassionate and inclusive society that values and prioritizes mental well-being for everyone.

Identifying common mental health challenges and disorders

Identifying and understanding common mental health challenges and disorders is essential for promoting early intervention and providing appropriate support. Here are some of the most prevalent mental health challenges and disorders:

Depression: Depression is a mood disorder characterized by persistent feelings of sadness, hopelessness, and a lack of interest or pleasure in activities. It can affect a person's thoughts, emotions, and behavior, leading to changes in sleep patterns, appetite, and energy levels. Major Depressive Disorder (MDD) is a common form of depression.

Anxiety Disorders: Anxiety disorders encompass a group of conditions characterized by excessive worry, fear, and nervousness. Generalized Anxiety Disorder (GAD), Social Anxiety Disorder, Panic Disorder, and Specific Phobias are examples of anxiety disorders. Individuals may experience physical symptoms like rapid heart rate, trembling, and sweating.

Bipolar Disorder: Bipolar Disorder involves periods of intense mood swings, including episodes of mania (elevated mood, high energy) and depression. Individuals may experience extreme highs and lows, affecting their ability to function and maintain stable relationships.

Schizophrenia: Schizophrenia is a severe and chronic mental disorder characterized by distorted thinking, hallucinations, delusions, disorganized speech, and diminished emotional expression. It often requires long-term treatment and support.

Post-Traumatic Stress Disorder (PTSD): PTSD develops after exposure to a traumatic event, such as physical violence, natural disasters, or combat. Individuals may experience flashbacks, nightmares, and hyper vigilance related to the trauma.

Obsessive-Compulsive Disorder (OCD): OCD involves recurring, intrusive thoughts (obsessions) that lead to repetitive behaviors or rituals (compulsions). Individuals engage in these rituals to alleviate anxiety and distress.

Eating Disorders: Eating disorders, such as Anorexia Nervosa, Bulimia Nervosa, and Binge Eating Disorder, are characterized by abnormal eating patterns and distorted body image. These disorders can lead to severe physical and psychological consequences.

Attention-Deficit/Hyperactivity Disorder (ADHD): ADHD is a neuro developmental disorder that affects attention, impulse control, and hyperactivity. It is typically diagnosed in childhood but can persist into adulthood.

Substance Use Disorders: Substance use disorders involve problematic use of alcohol, drugs, or other substances, leading to significant impairment in daily functioning and health.

Borderline Personality Disorder (BPD): BPD is a personality disorder characterized by unstable emotions, self-image, and relationships. Individuals may experience intense mood swings, fear of abandonment, and engage in impulsive behaviors.

Seasonal Affective Disorder (SAD): SAD is a type of depression that occurs seasonally, often during the fall and winter months when there is less natural sunlight. It is believed to be related to changes in light exposure.

It is essential to note that mental health challenges and disorders can manifest differently in each individual, and symptoms can vary in severity. Early recognition and intervention can significantly improve outcomes for those facing mental health issues. If you or someone you know is experiencing mental health challenges, seeking professional help from mental health practitioners, counselors, or psychiatrists is crucial for proper assessment and treatment.

Recognizing the signs and symptoms of different mental health   issues

Recognizing the signs and symptoms of different mental health issues can help identify potential challenges early and facilitate timely intervention. It is essential to remember that individuals may experience mental health conditions differently, and symptoms can vary in intensity. Here are some common signs and symptoms associated with different mental health issues:

Depression:

i. Persistent feelings of sadness, hopelessness, or emptiness.
ii. Loss of interest or pleasure in activities once enjoyed.
iii. Changes in appetite or weight (either loss or gain).
iv. Sleep disturbances, such as insomnia or oversleeping. Fatigue or lack of energy. Feelings of worthlessness or excessive guilt.
v. Difficulty concentrating or making decisions. Thoughts of death or suicide.

Anxiety Disorders:

i. Excessive worry or fear about various situations or events.
ii. Restlessness or feeling on edge.
iii. Rapid heart rate, trembling, or sweating.
iv. Difficulty controlling worry or intrusive thoughts.
v. Avoidance of situations that trigger anxiety.
vi. Panic attacks, characterized by sudden intense fear and physical symptoms like chest pain and shortness of breath.

Bipolar Disorder:

i. Periods of elevated mood (mania) characterized by increased energy, decreased need for sleep, and racing thoughts.
ii. Periods of depressive mood characterized by sadness, loss of interest, and fatigue.
iii. Rapid shifts in mood and energy levels.

Schizophrenia:

i.   Delusions, which are false beliefs not based on reality.

ii.   Hallucinations, such as hearing or seeing things that others don't.

iii.   Disorganized speech and behavior.

iv.   Reduced emotional expression and motivation.

Post-Traumatic Stress Disorder (PTSD):

i.   Intrusive thoughts or memories related to a traumatic event.

ii.   Nightmares or flashbacks of the traumatic experience.

iii.   Avoidance of triggers or reminders of the trauma.

iv.   Increased arousal and hyper vigilance.

Obsessive-Compulsive Disorder (OCD):

i.   Intrusive, unwanted thoughts or obsessions.

ii.   Compulsive behaviors or rituals performed to reduce anxiety related to the obsessions.

iii.   Feeling compelled to repeat certain actions or thoughts.

Eating Disorders:

i.   Drastic changes in eating patterns, such as restricting food intake or binge-eating.

ii.   Preoccupation with body weight, shape, and appearance.

iii.   Frequent trips to the bathroom after eating (indicative of purging behaviors).

Attention-Deficit/Hyperactivity Disorder (ADHD):

i.   Difficulty sustaining attention or completing tasks.

ii.   Impulsivity, acting without thinking about the consequences.

iii.   Hyperactivity, such as restlessness and constant fidgeting.

Borderline Personality Disorder (BPD):

i.   Unstable and intense relationships.

ii.   Impulsive behaviors, such as self-harm or substance abuse.

iii.   Mood swings and emotional instability.

iv.   Fear of abandonment.

Substance Use Disorders:

i.   Compulsive use of alcohol, drugs, or other substances despite negative consequences.

ii.   Withdrawal symptoms when attempting to stop using substances.

Recognizing these signs and symptoms is the first step toward supporting individuals facing mental health challenges. If you notice these symptoms in yourself or someone else, encourage seeking professional help from mental health experts. Early intervention and treatment can make a significant difference in managing mental health conditions and improving overall well-being.

BREAKING THE STIGMA

Addressing the stigma surrounding mental health and its negative impact

Addressing the stigma surrounding mental health is crucial for creating a more supportive and empathetic society that encourages individuals to seek help and support without fear of judgment. Stigma can be a significant barrier to people accessing mental health services and can have a negative impact on individuals facing mental health challenges. Here's how we can address mental health stigma and its negative impact:

Education and Awareness:

i. Promote education about mental health, mental illnesses, and the prevalence of these conditions in society.
ii. Organize awareness campaigns to debunk myths and misconceptions about mental health.
iii. Provide information on the signs and symptoms of mental health conditions to encourage early recognition and intervention.

Open Conversations:

i. Encourage open discussions about mental health in schools, workplaces, and communities.

ii. Create safe spaces for individuals to share their mental health experiences without judgment.

iii. Listen and validate the experiences of those facing mental health challenges.

Challenging Stereotypes:

i. Challenge media portrayals that reinforce stereotypes about mental health and individuals with mental illnesses.

ii. Highlight stories of recovery and resilience to counter negative narratives.

Language Matters:

i. Use person-first language that emphasizes the individual's humanity rather than defining them by their condition (e.g., "person with schizophrenia" instead of "schizophrenic").

ii. Avoid using derogatory terms or slurs related to mental health.

Leadership and Advocacy:

i. Promote mental health advocacy at all levels, from community organizations to government bodies.

ii. Encourage leaders to speak openly about mental health and lead by example in promoting understanding and support.

Integration of Mental Health and Physical Health Care:

i. Advocate for the integration of mental health care with primary health care services to reduce stigma and enhance accessibility to mental health support.

ii. Encourage health care professionals to discuss mental health as part of routine health check-ups.

Training and Sensitization:

i. Provide training and sensitization programs for professionals, educators, and the general public on mental health and stigma reduction.

ii.   Equip individuals with the knowledge and skills to support those with mental health challenges.

Role of Media and Celebrities:

i.   Encourage responsible media reporting on mental health, avoiding sensationalism or perpetuating stereotypes.

ii.   Engage celebrities and influencers to use their platforms to talk openly about mental health and promote understanding.

Support and Empathy:

i.   Offer support and empathy to individuals facing mental health challenges, letting them know they are not alone.

ii.   Recognize that mental health is an essential aspect of overall well-being and deserves the same level of care and compassion as physical health.

Addressing mental health stigma requires collective efforts from individuals, communities, and institutions. By fostering a more understanding and accepting environment, we can break down barriers to seeking help, improve access to mental health care, and support individuals on their journey to well-being and recovery.

Encouraging open conversations and reducing barriers to seeking help

Encouraging open conversations about mental health and reducing barriers to seeking help are essential steps in promoting mental health awareness and support. By creating a safe and understanding environment, we can empower individuals to share their experiences and seek assistance when needed. Here are some strategies to encourage open conversations and reduce barriers to mental health help:

Normalize Mental Health Discussions:

i.   Initiate conversations about mental health in everyday settings, such as schools, workplaces, and community gatherings.

   ii.   Share personal experiences or stories of mental health challenges to reduce stigma and encourage others to speak up.

Provide Mental Health Education:

   i.   Offer workshops, seminars, or educational programs to increase awareness and understanding of mental health issues.

   ii.   Teach students and employees about common mental health challenges, coping strategies, and available resources.

Create Safe Spaces:

   i.   Establish safe spaces where individuals can openly discuss their mental health without fear of judgment or discrimination.

   ii.   Ensure confidentiality and privacy to foster trust and openness.

Train Peer Supporters:

   i.   Train individuals to become peer supporters or mental health allies who can listen, offer support, and guide others to appropriate resources.

   ii.   Peer support can help reduce the sense of isolation and provide relatable assistance.

Use Online Platforms:

   i.   Utilize social media and online platforms to share mental health resources, personal stories, and positive messages.

   ii.   Online communities can be a source of support for those who may not feel comfortable sharing in-person.

Involve Leaders and Role Models:

   i.   Engage community leaders, public figures, and celebrities to openly discuss mental health.

   ii.   Their support and advocacy can have a significant impact on reducing stigma and inspiring others to seek help.

Employ Anti-Stigma Campaigns:

i. Launch anti-stigma campaigns to challenge stereotypes and promote empathy.

ii. Use engaging visuals and messages to convey the importance of mental health.

Make Help-Seeking Accessible:

i. Improve access to mental health services by reducing financial barriers and expanding mental health coverage in healthcare plans.

ii. Offer mental health services in schools, workplaces, and community centers for easy access.

Train Professionals on Cultural Competence:

i. Provide mental health professionals with cultural competence training to ensure they understand diverse perspectives and backgrounds.

ii. Culturally sensitive care can encourage individuals from different communities to seek help.

Encourage Early Intervention:

i. Emphasize the importance of early intervention and seeking help at the first signs of mental health challenges.

ii. Prompt action can prevent conditions from worsening and improve outcomes.

Promote Self-Care:

i. Encourage self-care practices and mental health well-being as a regular part of daily routines.

ii. Normalize the concept of taking care of mental health, just like physical health.

By implementing these strategies, we can foster an environment where mental health discussions are welcomed and where seeking help for mental health challenges is seen as a positive step toward well-being. Reducing barriers to mental health help and creating a supportive culture can lead to better mental health outcomes for individuals and a more empathetic and compassionate society as a whole.

Sharing stories of resilience and recovery to inspire hope and understanding

Sharing stories of resilience and recovery is a powerful way to inspire hope, reduce stigma, and foster understanding about mental health challenges. Personal narratives can create empathy and a sense of connection, letting others know that they are not alone in their struggles. Here's how sharing these stories can make a positive impact:

Reducing Stigma: Personal stories humanize mental health challenges and break down stereotypes. When individuals share their experiences of overcoming obstacles, it challenges the misconceptions surrounding mental health, promoting understanding and compassion.

Building Empathy: Hearing about the struggles and triumphs of others fosters empathy and a sense of shared humanity. It helps individuals understand the complexities of mental health issues and how they can impact different aspects of a person's life.

Offering Hope: Recovery stories serve as beacons of hope for those currently facing mental health challenges. Knowing that others have been through similar difficulties and have found their way to wellness can inspire individuals to seek help and believe in their own potential for recovery.

Encouraging Help-Seeking: When people hear stories of how seeking professional support has positively impacted others, it can encourage them to take the step to seek help for themselves or their loved ones.

Building Supportive Communities: Sharing stories within communities, workplaces, and schools can create supportive environments where people feel comfortable discussing mental health openly.

Fostering Connection: Personal stories encourage individuals to share their own experiences, leading to more open conversations and a sense of community among those with similar challenges.

Empowering Others: Individuals who share their stories often feel empowered by their ability to make a difference in the lives of others. It can be a transformative experience that strengthens their own recovery journey.

Raising Awareness: Personal stories serve as powerful advocacy tools, raising awareness about mental health issues and the need for accessible and compassionate mental health services.

Educating the Public: Sharing stories can educate the broader public about the complexity of mental health challenges and the importance of supporting mental health initiatives.

Encouraging Resilience: Resilience stories demonstrate the strength of the human spirit and the capacity to bounce back from adversity. They inspire others to develop resilience in their own lives.

When sharing personal stories, it's essential to respect individuals' privacy and consent. Some may choose to share anonymously, while others may be comfortable using their real names. Providing a safe and non-judgmental space for individuals to share their stories is crucial.

Overall, sharing stories of resilience and recovery plays a significant role in transforming attitudes toward mental health and promoting a more understanding and empathetic society. It reminds us that everyone's journey is unique, and with support and understanding, individuals facing mental health challenges can thrive and lead fulfilling lives.

MINDFULNESS AND MENTAL HEALTH

Introducing mindfulness practices for improved mental clarity and focus

Welcome to the world of mindfulness—a practice that can profoundly transform your mental clarity and focus, allowing you to live more fully in the present moment. In this fast-paced and often chaotic world, our minds can become cluttered with worries about the past or anxieties about the future. Mindfulness offers a path to anchor ourselves in the present and cultivate a sense of inner peace and clarity.

What is Mindfulness?

At its core, mindfulness is the art of being fully present and aware of our thoughts, feelings, bodily sensations, and the surrounding environment without judgment. It invites us to observe our experiences with curiosity and openness, acknowledging them without trying to change or suppress them. By practicing mindfulness, we learn to let go of distractions and tune into the richness of the present moment.

The Benefits of Mindfulness

Improved Mental Clarity: Mindfulness helps declutter the mind by gently redirecting our attention back to the present. This practice reduces mental chatter and enhances our ability to concentrate on the task at hand.

Heightened Focus: As we train our minds to focus on the present moment, we become better equipped to stay attentive and undistracted in our daily activities, leading to increased productivity and efficiency.

Stress Reduction: Mindfulness allows us to respond to stressors more skillfully by cultivating a calm and centered state of mind. By acknowledging stress without judgment, we can manage it more effectively.

Emotional Regulation: Practicing mindfulness helps us develop emotional intelligence, enabling us to recognize and understand our emotions without being overwhelmed by them.

Enhanced Self-Awareness: Mindfulness fosters self-awareness, leading to a deeper understanding of our thoughts, behaviors, and patterns. With this awareness, we can make conscious choices that align with our values.

Simple Mindfulness Practices for Clarity and Focus

Mindful Breathing: Take a few minutes each day to focus on your breath. Observe the sensation of each inhale and exhale, bringing your attention back to your breath whenever your mind wanders.

Body Scan: Practice a body scan by directing your attention through different parts of your body, noticing any sensations or tensions. This exercise helps bring you into the present moment and promotes relaxation.

Mindful Walking: During a walk, pay attention to each step, the feeling of your feet connecting with the ground, and the rhythm of your movements. Engage all your senses in the experience.

Mindful Eating: Savor each bite of your meals, paying attention to the taste, texture, and aroma. Eating mindfully can enhance your enjoyment of food and prevent overeating.

Mindful Listening: Practice active listening during conversations, fully focusing on the words, tone, and emotions conveyed by the speaker.

Mindful Technology Use: Be mindful of your screen time and use technology intentionally, setting aside designated periods for focus and limiting distractions.

Mindfulness is a transformative practice that can lead you to a greater sense of mental clarity, focus, and overall well-being. By embracing mindfulness in your daily life, you can cultivate a more balanced and meaningful existence, enriching your experiences and nurturing a deeper connection with yourself and the world around you. So, take a moment to pause, breathe, and embark on this journey of mindfulness an invaluable gift you can offer to yourself and those around you.

Practicing mindfulness meditation and relaxation techniques

Practicing mindfulness meditation and relaxation techniques can bring numerous benefits to your physical, mental, and emotional well-being. These practices help you become more aware of the present moment, reduce stress, and foster a sense of inner peace. Here's a step-by-step guide to get you started:

Find a Quiet Space: Choose a quiet and comfortable space where you won't be disturbed. It could be a corner of your home, a park, or any place where you feel at ease.

Sit or Lie Comfortably: Find a comfortable position, either sitting on a cushion or chair with your back straight, or lying down on your back. Keep your hands resting on your lap or by your sides.

Focus on Your Breath: Gently close your eyes and bring your attention to your breath. Notice the sensation of the breath as it enters and leaves your body. You can focus on the rise and fall of your abdomen or the feeling of air passing through your nostrils.

Observe Your Thoughts: As you meditate, you may notice thoughts arising in your mind. Instead of getting caught up in them, observe them like passing clouds without judgment. Bring your focus back to your breath whenever your mind wanders.

Body Scan: Another technique is the body scan. Slowly direct your attention through different parts of your body, starting from your toes and moving upwards. Notice any sensations, tension, or areas of relaxation.

Loving-Kindness Meditation: Practice loving-kindness meditation by silently repeating positive phrases like "May I be happy, may I be healthy, may I be at peace." Extend these wishes to yourself, loved ones, acquaintances, and even difficult people in your life.

Use Guided Meditations: If you find it challenging to meditate on your own, consider using guided meditation apps or recordings. These can lead you through mindfulness practices and relaxation exercises step by step.

Practice Regularly: Consistency is key to experiencing the benefits of mindfulness and relaxation techniques. Aim for at least a few minutes of practice daily or as often as you can manage.

Be Patient with Yourself: Mindfulness meditation is a skill that takes time to develop. Be patient with yourself and let go of expectations. There is no "right" or "wrong" way to meditate.

Integrate Mindfulness into Daily Life: As you become more familiar with mindfulness, try incorporating it into your daily activities. Practice mindful eating, walking, or simply pausing to take a few mindful breaths during the day.

 Remember, the goal of mindfulness is not to eliminate all thoughts but to cultivate awareness and acceptance of the present moment. Regular practice can lead to improved focus, reduced stress, and greater overall well-being. So, give yourself the gift of mindfulness and relaxation, and embrace the benefits it brings to your life.

Using mindfulness to manage anxiety, depression, and other mental health challenges

Mindfulness can be a powerful tool for managing anxiety, depression, and other mental health challenges. By cultivating awareness and non-judgmental acceptance of thoughts and emotions, mindfulness practices can help individuals develop healthier coping mechanisms and build resilience. Here's how mindfulness can be applied to manage these mental health challenges:

Anxiety:

Grounding Techniques: When anxiety becomes overwhelming, mindfulness can help by grounding yourself in the present moment. Focus on your breath, the sensation of your feet on the ground, or the sounds around you.

Observing Thoughts: Instead of getting caught up in anxious thoughts, practice observing them without judgment. Recognize that thoughts are not facts, and they will come and go.

Body Awareness: Tune into bodily sensations related to anxiety, such as tension or rapid heartbeat, and breathe into those areas to promote relaxation.

Acceptance: Embrace the feelings of anxiety without trying to push them away. Acceptance can lessen the resistance and make the anxiety more manageable.

Depression:

Gratitude Practice: Incorporate gratitude into your mindfulness routine. Reflect on positive aspects of life and find moments of joy or contentment, even in challenging times.

Self-Compassion: Treat yourself with kindness and compassion during periods of depression. Avoid self-criticism and remember that it's okay to have difficult emotions.

Mindful Movement: Engage in gentle physical activities like yoga or walking meditation to connect with your body and promote a sense of well-being.

Connection: Practice mindful social interactions, being fully present with others and seeking support from loved ones.

Emotional Regulation:

R.A.I.N. Technique: When experiencing strong emotions, use the R.A.I.N. technique - Recognize the emotion, Allow it to be present, Investigate the physical sensations and thoughts, and offer Non-identification by recognizing that emotions are not your identity.

Mindful Breathing: Employ deep breathing exercises to regulate emotions and create a sense of calm.

Three-Minute Breathing Space: When overwhelmed by emotions, take a three-minute break to focus on your breath and emotions without judgment.

Overall Mental Health:

Daily Practice: Establish a daily mindfulness routine to build resilience and improve overall mental well-being.

Mindful Self-Care: Prioritize self-care practices that foster mindfulness, such as journaling, spending time in nature, or engaging in creative activities.

Mindful Coping: When facing challenges, practice mindful coping techniques like the STOP exercise - Stop, Take a breath, Observe your thoughts and emotions, and Proceed mindfully.

Remember that mindfulness is a skill that develops over time with consistent practice. It may be helpful to work with a mental health professional or attend mindfulness-based therapy programs to deepen your understanding and integration of mindfulness into your life.

As you incorporate mindfulness into your mental health management, remember to be patient with yourself and approach the practice with an open mind and heart. Mindfulness can be a valuable companion on your journey toward greater well-being and emotional balance.

SELF-CARE AND WELL-BEING

The importance of self-care and its impact on mental health

Self-care is a crucial aspect of maintaining good mental health and overall well-being. It involves engaging in intentional activities and practices that promote physical, emotional, and psychological health. Self-care is not indulgence; rather, it is a necessary practice to nourish and recharge ourselves, especially in today's fast-paced and demanding world. Here's why self-care is essential and its positive impact on mental health:

Stress Reduction: Self-care activities, such as mindfulness, exercise, and relaxation techniques, can help reduce stress levels. Managing stress is vital for preventing the negative effects it can have on mental health.

Improved Emotional Well-Being: Taking time for self-care allows individuals to acknowledge and process their emotions in a healthy way. It fosters self-awareness and emotional intelligence, leading to better emotional regulation.

Increased Resilience: Engaging in self-care practices builds resilience by providing individuals with the tools to cope with life's challenges and bounce back from adversity.

Enhanced Self-Compassion: Self-care encourages individuals to treat themselves with kindness and compassion. Practicing self-compassion can reduce self-criticism and negative self-talk, leading to improved self-esteem.

Boundaries and Empowerment: Setting boundaries and prioritizing self-care empowers individuals to make decisions that align with their needs and values, reducing feelings of overwhelm and burnout.

Boosted Productivity: Taking breaks and practicing self-care can actually enhance productivity and focus. When individuals are well-rested and emotionally balanced, they perform better in their daily tasks.

Better Relationships: Self-care allows individuals to nurture themselves, which positively impacts their ability to be present and supportive in their relationships with others.

Prevention of Burnout: Regular self-care can prevent burnout, a state of emotional, physical, and mental exhaustion caused by prolonged stress and excessive demands.

Improved Physical Health: Self-care involves taking care of one's physical health, such as getting enough sleep, eating well, and engaging in regular exercise. Physical well-being is closely connected to mental health.

Mindfulness and Present-Moment Awareness: Self-care practices often involve mindfulness and present-moment awareness, which can reduce rumination about the past or worries about the future, leading to a greater sense of contentment.

Overall Life Satisfaction: Prioritizing self-care contributes to a greater sense of life satisfaction and happiness. It allows individuals to lead a more balanced and fulfilling life.

Remember that self-care is unique to each individual. What works for one person may not work for another, and it's essential to find self-care practices that resonate with you. Whether it's spending time in nature, engaging in creative pursuits, practicing meditation, or simply taking time for yourself, regular self-care can have a profound and positive impact on your mental health and well-being. So, make self-care a priority and invest in nurturing yourself— your mind, body, and soul.

Developing a personalized self-care routine for physical and mental well-being

Developing a personalized self-care routine is a wonderful way to prioritize your physical and mental well-being. The key is to choose activities and practices that resonate with you and bring you joy and relaxation. Here are some steps to help you create your own self-care routine:

Reflect on Your Needs and Preferences: Take some time to reflect on the activities and practices that make you feel good and rejuvenated. Consider what brings you joy, peace, and a sense of well-being. It could be anything from spending time in nature, reading a book, practicing yoga, or enjoying a hobby.

Identify Your Goals: Think about what you want to achieve with your self-care routine. It could be stress reduction, improved sleep, enhanced focus, or simply a better sense of balance in your life.

Set Realistic Time Commitments: Be mindful of your schedule and commitments. Ensure that your self-care activities fit comfortably within your daily routine. Even small pockets of time can be valuable for self-care.

Create a Daily or Weekly Plan: Based on your reflections, goals, and available time, create a self-care plan. Decide on the frequency and duration of each activity. It can be helpful to set aside specific time slots for self-care in your calendar.

Balance Physical and Mental Practices: Include a mix of activities that promote both physical and mental well-being. For physical self-care, consider exercise, stretching, or mindful movement. For mental well-being, incorporate meditation, mindfulness, or journaling.

Be Open to Experimentation: Self-care is a personal journey, and it may take some trial and error to find what works best for you. Be open to trying new activities and adjust your routine as needed.

Stay Consistent: Consistency is key to reaping the benefits of self-care. Aim to practice your routine regularly, even if it's just for a few minutes each day.

Be Mindful and Present: Approach your self-care activities with mindfulness and present-moment awareness. Allow yourself to fully immerse in the experience without distractions.

Include Social Connections: Consider incorporating social activities into your routine. Spending quality time with loved ones and nurturing meaningful relationships can be a vital aspect of self-care.

Prioritize Rest and Sleep: Ensure that your self-care routine includes sufficient time for rest and quality sleep. Adequate rest is essential for both physical and mental rejuvenation.

Practice Self-Compassion: Remember that self-care is not about perfection or adding more stress to your life. Be kind to yourself and practice self-compassion if your routine needs adjustments or if you miss a day.

Remember that self-care is an ongoing process, and your routine can evolve over time as your needs change. The key is to make self-care a priority and to create a routine that nourishes your mind, body, and soul, allowing you to thrive and find balance in your daily life.

Balancing work, life, and leisure to promote overall wellness

Balancing work, life, and leisure is essential for promoting overall wellness and maintaining a healthy and fulfilling lifestyle. Striking this balance allows you to manage stress, prevent burnout, and enhance your physical and mental well-being. Here are some strategies to help you achieve a harmonious balance:

Set Clear Boundaries: Establish clear boundaries between work and personal time. Define specific work hours and try to stick to them, allowing yourself to disconnect and focus on other aspects of life during non-work hours.

Prioritize Self-Care: Make self-care a priority in your daily routine. Schedule time for activities that promote physical and mental well-being, such as exercise, meditation, hobbies, or spending time with loved ones.

Practice Time Management: Use effective time management techniques to make the most of your work hours. Prioritize tasks, set realistic deadlines, and avoid multitasking, which can lead to decreased productivity and increased stress.

Limit Technology Use: Reduce unnecessary screen time and limit the use of digital devices during leisure hours. Disconnecting from work-related emails and notifications can help you unwind and be fully present in your personal life.

Plan Leisure Activities: Schedule leisure activities and make them non-negotiable parts of your week. Whether it's spending time outdoors, reading a book, or engaging in a creative pursuit, dedicating time to leisure is crucial for well-being.

Delegate and Seek Support: If possible, delegate tasks at work and seek support in your personal life when needed. Sharing responsibilities can free up time for other essential aspects of life.

Learn to Say No: Be mindful of taking on additional commitments that may overwhelm you. Learn to say no to tasks or obligations that may interfere with your work-life balance.

Create a Supportive Work Environment: If you have the flexibility, consider discussing work-life balance with your employer or supervisor. A supportive work environment can encourage employees to maintain a healthy balance.

Be Present in the Moment: Whether you're at work, spending time with loved ones, or enjoying leisure activities, practice being fully present in the moment. Mindfulness can enhance your experience and reduce unnecessary stress.

Regularly Assess and Adjust: Regularly assess how you are managing work, life, and leisure. Be open to adjusting your approach as needed to maintain a healthy balance.

Remember that achieving work-life-leisure balance is an ongoing process. It requires continuous effort and a willingness to adapt as life circumstances change. By prioritizing overall wellness and making conscious choices, you can create a fulfilling and balanced life that promotes both personal and professional growth and happiness.

SEEKING PROFESSIONAL HELP

Knowing when to seek professional support for mental health concerns

Knowing when to seek professional support for mental health concerns is essential for early intervention and effective management of mental health challenges. Here are some indicators that may suggest it's time to reach out to a mental health professional:

Persistent or Intense Symptoms: If you experience persistent or intense emotional, behavioral, or cognitive symptoms that interfere with your daily life, it's important to seek professional help. These symptoms may include prolonged sadness, anxiety, mood swings, or difficulty concentrating.

Impaired Functioning: If you find it challenging to perform daily activities, fulfill responsibilities at work or school, or maintain healthy relationships due to your mental health symptoms, professional support can be beneficial.

Thoughts of Self-Harm or Suicide: If you have thoughts of self-harm or suicide, it is crucial to seek immediate help. Reach out to a mental health professional, a crisis hotline, or go to the nearest emergency room.

Sudden Changes in Behavior: Significant changes in behavior, such as increased irritability, social withdrawal, or substance abuse, may indicate an underlying mental health concern that requires professional evaluation.

Difficulty Coping with Stress: If you find it challenging to cope with stress, anxiety, or overwhelming emotions, a mental health professional can provide tools and strategies to manage these challenges effectively.

Loss of Interest and Pleasure: If you have lost interest in activities you once enjoyed or are experiencing a persistent lack of pleasure in life, it may be a sign of depression or other mental health issues.

Sleep Disturbances: Chronic insomnia or changes in sleep patterns can be indicative of underlying mental health concerns and may warrant professional evaluation.

Relationship Conflicts: If you are experiencing persistent conflicts or challenges in your personal or professional relationships, seeking therapy or counseling can be helpful in improving communication and resolving issues.

Past Trauma or Grief: If you have experienced past trauma or are struggling to cope with grief and loss, professional support can be instrumental in processing emotions and finding healing.

Intuition or Concern from Loved Ones: If family members, friends, or colleagues express concerns about your well-being or behavior, it's essential to consider their observations and seek professional support if necessary.

Remember, seeking help from a mental health professional is a sign of strength, not weakness. Mental health professionals are trained to provide support, guidance, and evidence-based treatments to help you navigate mental health challenges and improve your overall well-being.

Navigating the process of therapy and counseling

Navigating the process of therapy and counseling can feel overwhelming, especially if it's your first time seeking professional support for your mental health. However, with some understanding and preparation, you can make the process more comfortable and productive. Here are some steps to help you navigate therapy and counseling:

Identify Your Needs: Reflect on why you are seeking therapy or counseling. Identify the specific concerns or challenges you want to address. This will help you communicate your needs to the mental health professional.

Research and Find a Suitable Therapist: Look for therapists or counselors who specialize in the areas you want to work on. You can search online, ask for recommendations from friends or family, or contact mental health organizations in your area.

Schedule an Initial Consultation: Many therapists offer free or low-cost initial consultations. Use this opportunity to ask questions, discuss your concerns, and get a sense of whether the therapist's approach aligns with your needs.

Establish Goals and Expectations: Clarify your therapy goals and discuss them with the therapist. Establish realistic expectations for the therapeutic process and understand that progress may take time.

Understand the Therapeutic Approach: Ask the therapist about their therapeutic approach and methods. This will help you understand what to expect during sessions and how the therapist plans to address your concerns.

Discuss Confidentiality and Boundaries: Understand the therapist's confidentiality policy and the limits of confidentiality. Knowing that your sessions are confidential can help you feel more comfortable sharing openly.

Be Open and Honest: During therapy sessions, be open and honest with your therapist. Honesty is essential for effective therapy and can lead to better insights and understanding.

Engage in the Process: Engage actively in the therapy process. Completing homework assignments or practicing strategies discussed in sessions can help reinforce progress.

Be Patient and Allow Progress: Therapy is a journey, and progress may not be linear. Be patient with yourself and trust the process. Celebrate small victories along the way.

Provide Feedback: If something doesn't feel right or if you have concerns about the therapy, communicate openly with your therapist. Honest feedback can lead to adjustments that better suit your needs.

Know When to Seek a Different Therapist: If you find that you don't feel comfortable or connected with your therapist after giving it a fair chance, it's okay to seek another therapist who may be a better fit for you.

Remember that therapy is a collaborative process, and finding the right therapist for you is essential. Trust your instincts and take the time to find a mental health professional who you feel comfortable working with. Therapy and counseling can be transformative experiences, helping you navigate life's challenges and improve your mental and emotional well-being.

CONCLUSION

As we conclude our journey together, remember that nurturing mental health is an ongoing process. By embracing the knowledge gained from this guide, you possess the power to foster a healthier and more fulfilling life. Embrace the journey with compassion, self-awareness, and resilience, knowing that seeking help is a sign of strength, not weakness. Together, let us work toward building a society that prioritizes mental health and fosters a culture of empathy and understanding. May you find joy, peace, and well-being as you continue on your path of self-discovery and mental wellness.

ABOUT THE AUTHOR

Okafor Emmanuel Onyedika,
I'm a compassionate and knoledgeable personal deeply committed to promoting well-being. With a profound understanding of mental health, i offer insightful advice and practical strategies for achieving emotional balance and resilience. Through my expertise, empathy, and genuine desire to help others, my guide becomes an invaluable resource for anyone seeking to prioritize and enhance their mental well-being